MW00422700

Car Care for the Clueless:

Successful Used Car Buying 101

By Pamela Oakes,
ASE-certified technician and auto dealer

A Pumpkin Pie Production
Oakes Entertainment

Copyright © 2012 Pamela Oakes
All Rights Reserved

ISBN-10: 0615579663
ISBN-13: 9780615579665

Index

Intro

Some car ads call it "pre-loved" and other say call it "pre-owned." But let's just call it what it is: a used vehicle. Someone had the vehicle before you looked at it on a car lot. The previous owner either didn't like something about it or—and this is important—there was something mechanically wrong with the car or truck. It could have been a mysterious auto ailment, or the repair cost was too much for the old owner.

After you read this book, I am sure that when you look at your new car or truck sitting in the driveway, you'll say, "I'm really happy that I bought this vehicle."

- Pam

Chapter 1:
Time for a change

So, you don't like your car.

You would rather have a silver crossover than that green minivan. You just really hate looking at the one-time red, but now pinkish blob that's waiting for you at the end of each workday. Boy, what you wouldn't give for a black sports car. Is it economically feasible to trade now, or should you wait for a better financial opportunity. In other words, what's your car worth? How much can you get for your trade?

A vehicle is one of the biggest investments that you will make in your lifetime. So why not treat it as such? The key is to get the most car for your cash. They say knowledge is power. And this includes knowing how to play the crazy games of the car sales industry. There is no time like the present, so let's get started.

First we are going to talk about those of you who are on the fence about getting a newer used vehicle. But for others—the ones have no choice but to replace their car or truck due to a wreck or catastrophic breakdown—don't go too far. I will be back with you soon.

You hear commercials on the radio and see ads on television: "Get Top Dollar for Your Trade." So, what does that mean? Does it mean the dealer is going to give you more than what it's worth?

No.

Does it mean you don't have to negotiate for your vehicle's optimum value?

Not only no, but hell no!

Remember: there is no such thing as a free lunch or a free tire...and getting top dollar for your vehicle trade-in.

It's all about the numbers, and unfortunately, most people aren't car savvy when it comes to wheeling and dealing car contracts. But you will be.

First, though, we need to find out how much your current vehicle is worth. There are multiple publications and online resources about this. Basically, vehicles vary in value. And those values are skewed due to "cash for clunkers" and the state of our national economy. There is the "black book" value for your vehicle, but this car value guide is available to car dealers, only. And they update this publication very often. So, who really knows how much your car is worth? How do you put a price tag on it?

First, check with your insurance agent. They have put a monetary value on your car or truck. Explain that you are thinking about selling your automobile but are unsure of the "actual" value. Then ask our agent this: if you hypothetically wrecked your vehicle today, how much would the company say its worth is? Please emphasize that you do not plan to wreck the car or truck. You are looking for a monetary value for negotiating purposes only. At the same time, you can ask your agent how much your premium will be for a newer vehicle.

Between the insurance company's estimate and those you compile from books and online sources, you have a very good idea of your vehicle's value.

Let's step back for a moment. At this point, we have a good guess of what your ride is worth. Now ask yourself, *Am I "upside down" with my vehicle?* You know what I'm talking about: do you owe more than what it's worth? Before continuing on with your quest, take into consideration all the financial ramifications that this could create for your credit score—and your checking account.

Make sure that buying a newer used car won't hurt your budget.

NOTES:

NOTES:

NOTES:

NOTES:

Chapter 2:
Look past the bells and whistles

It's time to take a hard, honest look at your ride. Let's start with the exterior. Has it been damaged from a previous wreck? Does it need a paint job? Is the paint dull from lack of wax? You've heard about first impressions, right? Well, this is the first impression that your vehicle is going to give the receiving dealership. They are looking at all these issues and are immediately deducting the repair from what they intend to give you for the car.

If you want to know how much body work is needed, get an estimate from a respected body shop. Having talked to a bump shop, you may find that all it needs is an exterior refinish—in a color you prefer—to give it that "new car" feel. But you need to have the mechanical portion checked over before pouring money in this vehicle that you are considering trading.

Go to a reputable ASE–Blue Seal shop. Ask how much it costs to have a vehicle checked over for purchase. Ask the service adviser for a list of components that are inspected. Does it cover the tires, brakes, or hoses? Does it check drivability issues too?

No warning lights illuminated on your dash? No light, no problem, right? Wrong! Computers can be reset, and sensors and actuators can be rigged to fool a computer. Have your vehicle checked out thoroughly. Just when I think I have seen it all, something else pops up that someone has "rigged" in an attempt to pass inspection.

Now, let's look at the interior. Is the upholstery ripped? What's the condition of the arm rests? Is the steering wheel worn? Is the floor cluttered with junk; is the trunk cluttered with junk? Automotive upholstery shops can give you an estimate—after the interior has been cleaned—for repairs needed to make the inside look new.

Take all three of these factors: interior, exterior, and mechanical repairs, and subtract that from your vehicle's value. If the repairs exceed the value of the vehicle, it's time to move on.

Why? Because you don't want to put money into a vehicle that would put your checkbook in the red. You need to get a return on your repairs, paint, or interior work.
There is another factor to consider: What if you absolutely, positively cannot purchase another vehicle at this time?

Well, if you are in this situation, I recommend having your vehicle checked over for safety at an ASE–Blue Seal shop by an ASE-certified technician. Have him or her go bumper to bumper checking all safety items—items that are needed to guarantee safe travel to and from work, home, etc.

You must communicate with the shop how the vehicle is used and in what conditions. For example: you use your car only within city limits and in stop and go traffic, or you drive it long distance on the highway to commute. They need to know this to properly inspect your vehicle. There are several factors for an ASE-certified technician to consider if you are a "normal" or "severe" duty driver. This information will allow him or her to give you a more exact evaluation.

Then have the ASE–Blue Seal Shop itemize the repairs—if needed—in order of importance. Have the safety repairs completed. Leave the cosmetic items for the next owner. Doing makes the car safe, but you won't be pouring money into a vehicle that is below its value.

Used vehicles are priced at a premium, thanks to "cash for clunkers." The values are skewed, and the average car lot is taking advantage of the situation. Therefore, there is a second factor that you may want to consider before trading in your old jalopy.

For example, a customer of mine has two teenaged children. The first teenager is driving a hand-me-down vehicle, but has saved money from her part-time job to purchase her "dream car." About a month before she was to have the funds to purchase the vehicle, the hand-me-down suffered a mechanical failure, and the engine sustained irreversible damage. (Note: Check your engine oil level regularly.) The second teenager was to inherit this vehicle, but now it needs an engine. I suggested the following, since the vehicle owner had records of its repair history—and they were few— and the vehicle was cosmetically clean inside and out: it would benefit him to replace the engine. I know, even though the cost of the repairs would exceed the vehicle's value, but in this case it would benefit the car owner's wallet by having the second teenager hone his or her driving skills on the hand-me-down.

Each case is different. So, do your homework and make sure you factor in a good dose of common sense.

So, let's move on.

NOTES:

NOTES:

NOTES:

NOTES:

LOOK PAST THE BELLS AND WHISTLES

NOTES:

Chapter 3:
The search is on for your next vehicle

This is the chapter where both situations—wanting to buy a car and needing to buy a car—collide. You are either someone who is looking for a used car or someone who is in need of a used car due to an accident.

Before you choose your dream machine, you need to consider how much you can afford for a down payment. And let's not forget about that monthly loan payment. Your first step is to run your credit report. Of course, everybody knows that the higher your credit rating, the better interest rate. Now is the time to choose between financing the vehicle through a banking institution and utilizing the dealership for funding. You can get a good idea of the going interest rate by checking out various free Internet programs. Don't forget that they may ask about your credit rating. (Note: Never give out personal information on the Internet unless you know exactly who is receiving it.)

The payments work like this: The financial group breaks it down by the loan amount versus how much time. Generally, the more time you take to pay off the loan, the lower the payment. On the flip side, you will be paying more for the vehicle in the long run. Make sure you don't get caught about four years from now, when you are ready to trade, being "upside down" in your vehicle. Owing more than the car is worth is what gets individuals in financial difficulties.

It's always best to have your financing in place before you make a vehicle purchase. Car buyers often can get a better rate by preplanning. Be a good scout, and be prepared before going into the lobby of a car lot. And don't tell the dealership how much you want to spend on your monthly payments. If you do, you will most likely miss out on "last minute" rebates, incentives, or other deals. If a dealer knows how much money he or she can take out of your wallet, that's how much you are going to pay for the car.

Now that you have your financing in order, the fun begins. It's time to pick out the car or truck of your dreams. This is a very, very important step. You want to make sure that when you are seated in a vehicle, it makes a smile come over your face. But, at the same time, you need to find a vehicle that will suit your everyday activities. If you're a soccer mom or dad, you may want to look at a minivan or a crossover. A college student may want to consider a small economy car. If you're just starting out, a four-door may suit you better. And if you do any towing, a pickup truck may be the option for you. It is important that you really pay attention to your needs and those required in your new wheels. The worst thing that could happen is choosing a vehicle only to realize later on that you need another type of car or truck. You need to take a look at all the activities you do daily and figure out what type of vehicle is going to take you down the road.

There are dozens and dozens of makes and models out there for you to choose from. Everyone has a favorite, but keep an open mind about other vehicle options. And someone who's been driving a foreign four-door sedan for the past ten years may be ready for two-door domestic sports coupe.

So, let's find you a vehicle.

NOTES:

NOTES:

NOTES:

NOTES:

NOTES:

Chapter 4:
A few of your favorite things

Believe it or not, it's good to choose your top four favorite colors. This is important because for the next four to six years you will be looking at the color you choose. If you don't like the color of your car or truck, you're likely going to end up abusing the vehicle. When you hate the car, you're not going to maintain it—and that attitude cost money. Also, keep in mind that certain colors are unpopular (depending on the manufacturer and model). If you are okay with those colors, you may get a better deal. To find which vehicles sport the most popular colors, look in any annual auto almanac or online search engine.

Just as you chose the colors for your truck or car, you need to choose what type of options will suit your everyday needs. Even though you may not be a great fan of a minivan, it may be what matches your activities. But step back, and take a second look at things. You need the versatility of a minivan, but maybe a crossover can do the job too. Humm. Remember to keep in mind the activities you do daily or weekly. How much room will you need? How many people will you be transporting? How many miles per day and per week will you be driving? These are all important questions you need to ask yourself.

For example, a four-door sedan that seats five is not going to help you if you are a soccer parent and are expected to pick up and drop off children. On the other hand, an older couple with an empty nest probably doesn't need the extra room of a minivan.

Fuel economy also plays a huge role in what type of vehicle you purchase. There are several websites available that give you approximate, miles per gallon (mpg). Remember, these are only estimates. These figures are from a closed-course roadway with a professional driver. Your personal driving techniques will dictate your MPG in any vehicle.

For example, a four-door sedan was driven by two separate people. For the first week, the first person drove the vehicle to and from work, the grocery store, etc. This person did not wait for the last second to brake when the light turned red. Also, he didn't do "jack rabbit" starts. On the second week, the second driver took over the same vehicle. She too went to work, the grocery store, etc. and was a little more aggressive with in-town traffic. But she used the vehicle's cruise control whenever possible. Also, she made sure that the proper air pressure was in the tires and that the fuel gauge did not go below a quarter of a tank. The second driver actually got two miles more per gallon than the first driver.

How is this you ask?

She did all the proper things to getting better fuel economy. It doesn't matter which make or model, or the type of vehicle. These are key ingredients to make your car go farther on a tank of gas.

Now let's choose a car for you.

Okay, we have your color. We have your make and model. Now it's time to narrow the selection. (Trust me, this will all be worth it in the end.) There are dozens and dozens of websites with cars and trucks for sale. Local convenience stores have weekly circulars that also have cars and trucks for sale. The newspaper even has car dealership ads. With all these options, there is no reason we can't find your dream car. So let's check and see if what you're looking for is even within your price range.

The easiest way to start is by searching the web. Whatever search engine you choose, there will be dozens and dozens of your dream vehicle for sale. Don't be overwhelmed by all the options. Remember, you want to find a vehicle within your price range. And don't forget to choose a driving radius that you feel comfortable traveling. I recommend choosing five vehicle options to ensure a successful sale.

Also remember that you're on a mission to find *your* car. Don't get off track by other vehicle sales or offers.

I had a neighbor who was in a traffic accident; his vehicle was totaled. He needed a car—now. He knew he needed a four-door sedan, but a salesperson tried to convince him that he "looked better" in a two-door roadster. (Later we found out that the roadster had been on the lot for too long, so the dealership wanted it sold.) But he did the right thing and insisted that he was going to purchase the vehicle he had intended to buy before he walked onto the lot. Remember this example and concentrate on your choices. Tunnel vision will help make your vehicle purchase a success-ful venture.

You have your five vehicle options. It's time to take each model for a test drive, which I highly recommend. Even if you own an earlier version of one of the choice models, never assume that it's the same vehicle. Newer versions have changes that you may not want in your new vehicle.

For example, I had a customer who wanted to upgrade his vehicle by two years—same make and model—only to find that the cabin space was six inches shorter than his previous vehicle. Because he was very tall, the newer version was very uncomfortable to drive. Fortunately, he took my advice and test drove it. If he had not followed through this process, this would have been a very expensive, long-lasting lesson— a four- to six-year lesson. How horrible would that have been?

Now let's narrow your choices.

NOTES:

NOTES:

NOTES:

NOTES:

NOTES:

NOTES:

Chapter 5:
Research: Finding the right fit

Now that you have your five choices, it's time to see which ones you can afford. It doesn't matter if you are looking for a high-priced or an economy vehicle, they all have their quirks. Common items may break or need regular maintenance on certain models.

For example, you need to find out if the vehicle has a timing belt or a timing chain. It's the timing belt or chain's job to keep the internal engine components in sync with each other. The timing belt is made of a rubber composite and needs to be replaced on a regular basis. The timing chain is made of a metal composite and does not need to be replaced regularly. A timing belt can cost between 500 and 950 dollars, parts and labor. There is no set schedule for a timing chain replacement. The preventive, timed maintenance cost for a chain is zero dollars.

Some vehicles have brake components that must be exchanged when a front or rear brake job is performed. Most rotors can be resurfaced, but some models require replacing the rotors during each brake-pad exchange. On some models, this can cost up to six hundred dollars per axle (either the front or rear set of wheels). On models on which you don't have to replace the rotors each time, the brake pad, resurface rotors, and labor should be around 225 dollars per axle.

You also will eventually have to replace the spark plugs. Most vehicles take platinum spark plugs. (Note: remember to replace the spark plug with like kind—if it is an AC-Delco plug, replace it with an AC-Delco plug. If an NGK plug came out, replace it with an NGK one. Try to keep your vehicle as original as possible. Auto parts stores upselling you product may not benefit you but only the store's bottom line.)

Spark plug prices can range from eight to twelve dollars. Then there are the double-platinum and iridium plugs. These can cost from twelve to twenty-four dollars each. An engine may use four, six, or eight spark plugs. Well, actually, a couple of eight-cylinder models have an exhaust spark plug, so they require sixteen spark plugs. Oh, did I mention that they may require ignition wires or boots? They can range from twelve dollars each boot; seventy-five dollars for a decent wire set. But, then again, most vehicles have the "coil over plug" setup. That means each spark plug has its own power source: an ignition coil. These coils can range from 75 to 125 dollars each. Multiply that by six or eight, and add the installation labor. This all adds up to subtracting money from your wallet. It may be boring research for you, but just think of the things you can do with that extra cash.

You can make this a stress-free project by simply asking your ASE-certified technician.

Now, let's talk about tires. Do the vehicles on your list require a regular touring tire or a speed-rated tire? A regular, touring tire can range from eighty to one hundred dollars for a decent tire. A performance tire can go—easily—past the two hundred-dollar mark—for each tire. Then there is the tire size. If you have a simple 1500 series pickup, it still can require an extra-load tire on some models. You need to know how much those sneakers are going to zap your checking account.

Then there is the size of the tire. Is it a seventeen- or eighteen-inch? Or did you pick out the fancy rims and tires that start around twenty-two inches? The larger the tire diameter, the larger the tire bill. So, this is another place to check for future repair costs.

Some of the vehicles have software for trouble shooting. This is going to cost more at a dealership than at a reliable ASE–Blue Seal independent shop. So, find out if your vehicle choices require that special service.

Last but not least, ask your ASE-certified technician—the trusted tech that you take your present vehicle to for repairs—which cars that they like or dislike. Tell them to elaborate on why they favor a particular vehicle over another. And remember, this is just an opinion. All technicians have their favorite manufacturer, so remind them that you want them to help you regarding the repair aspect. Ask them for a copy of the trouble service bulletin (TSB) list for each choice, along with the manufacturer's recall list. Your tech can give you a manufacturer supplied maintenance schedule from either program, as well. These items will help you with your final choice.

All of this footwork will save you money in repairs and maintenance, so take the time to do your comparison homework. Just think what you can do with that extra green—a great vacation, a savings account, new golf clubs, or a new wardrobe.

Now it's time to test drive your dream car.

NOTES:

NOTES:

NOTES:

NOTES:

NOTES:

Chapter 6:

Ready, set, test drive

OK, you made your semifinal choice. Let's see if it fits your lifestyle.

Ask the dealer if renting the car for twenty-four hours is an option. They will require some type of deposit and personal information. This makes sense. The car dealer wants to protect his property, his investment. If that particular dealership does not provide that type of service, see if a rental car is an option for you. Various rental agencies allow you to choose your make and model. Explain to the rental agent that you want to see if this make and model is a good fit for you. Also, rent-a-car companies sell vehicles, so ask them if they have your particular make and model available for purchase as well.

Don't bypass the extended test-drive process. Keep in mind the story regarding the tall man looking to purchase a vehicle. He would have purchased the newer car with less legroom—what a horrible mistake!

So, you're in your vehicle. It's time to take a look around and check out the amenities. Is it easy for you to get in and out of the car? Do you like the steering wheel position, or can it be tilted to the angle you desire? If it's a van, does it have front and rear air-conditioning? If you had front and rear climate control in your old van, can you live without this convenience? Can you adjust the driver's seat for safety and comfort? Does it have automatic door locks on the key fob for safety?

I drive different car and truck models every day. And difference in the vehicle year and options can mean different interior changes. It could be something as silly as the arm rest being moved an inch or two. To some people, this is a big deal. Some vehicles may have the arm rests in different positions; others may have a larger center console that interferes with some drivers' accelerator leg position.

This is just the tip of the iceberg. These are just some of the items that you need to check out in your new, used vehicle.

Remember, you're not purchasing this test vehicle. The reason for this ride is to see if you fit well in this make and model year. Your list of comfort options is going to be for your actual purchase. Don't get the two confused. You don't want to miss a great vehicle opportunity because you are swayed by the options on a rent-a-car versus what you can afford in your dream machine version.

Let's locate your choice car.

NOTES:

NOTES:

NOTES:

NOTES:

NOTES:

NOTES:

Chapter 7:

Hide and seek: Where to find your dream car

Now you have your used vehicle selection down to two. It's always good to have a backup vehicle choice. You want to have these two options due to availability and price.

There are multiple ways to choose a used car. Traditionally, people us newspaper ads and car magazines. These are available at the corner convenience store. Although not as popular as they once were, they can be a valuable source. Some dealerships like to place ads in these with special pricing and coupons so they can see if their print advertisements are working.

Then there is the Internet. *Caveat emptor* (buyer, beware).

A friend of the family's was looking for a car for their daughter. Of course, the daughter, being Internet savvy, went straight to a well-known website that sells more than cars. After she found her dream car, she made the first call to the sellers. They were more than anxious to take a deposit—over the phone! Since her parents were financing the vehicle, she showed them the photos of the car online. Between the three sets of eyes, someone noticed that there was something very wrong with the listed car. But the photos of its exterior were matched with the interior for another car—not even from the same car manufacturer. When the daughter called the owners and asked about the difference, they told her that the interior photos were correct. This bogus sale was even more evident when she called again and the phone had been disconnected.

This is why you do your homework. The person who bought this vehicle sight unseen would have learned an expensive lesson learned. He would have had a nasty reality check as his car money just went to a mystery Internet car hundreds of miles away.

Always, always, always make sure you physically see the vehicle before making a *refundable* deposit. You want to make double sure that it is a refundable deposit. The best way to make a deposit on a vehicle is via check or credit card—*no cash!* With those options, you have a record of your deposit. If you change your mind and want your deposit back, there is a record of the transaction.

Another scam is the over-the-phone sale of the car you're getting rid of. The individual tells you that he is sending you a check more than the value of the car. You are to take that extra money and pay for the shipping. You sign over the car title. The transport hauler takes your car. Then, about a week later, you find out that the seller's check is bogus. Now you are out of the shipping cost—and a car!

Then we have the local, used-car dealerships. They generally get their stock for sale from auto auctions. As in all products, there are several categories of vehicles: poor, fair, good, better, and best. The higher the quality of the vehicle, the better your chances that it will serve you well in the future. Dealerships advertise online, in the newspapers, on television, and on the radio. In most circumstances, they are regulated by local and/or state agencies. Therefore they are more accountable for the process regarding paperwork of the vehicle sale than the vehicle's condition. So it is still the buyer's responsibility to confirm the quality of the car or truck.

Another vehicle purchase choice is the private seller. This is an independent person who wants to get the most out of his car sale and is looking for the most money. The majority of these honest, hardworking car owners want to sell their vehicle to purchase a newer model used—or a new—vehicle. Most times, private vehicle sellers are unaware that there is anything wrong with their car or truck. They rely on the garage or shade-tree mechanic for maintenance.

Why risk your safety and money?

NOTES:

NOTES:

NOTES:

NOTES:

NOTES:

Chapter 8:
Check it out for safety

No matter how nice the present owner of the vehicle is or how much maintenance paperwork he provides—you need to have the vehicle checked out before you consider purchase. Don't take it to the seller's choice of a repair shop. Take it to your repair facility, or if you are out of town, to an ASE–Blue Seal shop. Just be sure to take the vehicle to someone not familiar with it. You want a fresh set of eyes checking out your new ride. Remember, you will be paying for this safety inspection, so remind the technician checking out your prospective vehicle that he is working for you, not for the owner of the vehicle. There are more times than I care to remember when the owner of a used vehicle has talked to me or another one of my technicians, trying to make us believe that his vehicle was in superior working order—and it was anything but.

One time I had a used-car dealer tell me that my insurance did not cover me to test drive a vehicle. I explained to the salesperson that my shop and I were covered and took it on a test drive. Thank goodness I did. After the engine warmed up, the car did not shift properly, which indicated definite transmission issues. I explained to my customer—the prospective buyer—that the transmission was not shifting correctly. I also could tell that someone had recently erased the engine codes (there was a P1000, telling me all vehicle systems had not passed the system tests since the most recent reset). Most likely, an unscrupulous person disconnected the battery or PCM fuse to reset the system. So, what else was going on with the car? We told the potential car purchaser to keep looking.

I have had sellers attempt to bribe my staff and me to overlook certain items. They would tell us that it would be "worth it" not to check certain systems on the vehicle they were selling. But, as I remind everyone involved—seller and buyer—my job is to inspect the vehicle for purchase. I present my findings, and it is up to both parties to decide what comes next: negotiations or choosing another vehicle.

Oh, here's another automotive horror story. A family friend was transferred out of the area. He needed a newer used vehicle—fast. He found a high-end, European vehicle online and purchased it from the nationally known dealership. The dealership said that the vehicle had a 106-point inspection and checked out okay. The family friend drove the vehicle on the interstate for about ninety miles. The oil light come on at about the same time the vehicle was approaching the interstate exit. He came over to my shop and had me check it. Not only was the vehicle low on oil, the oil was *black*.! (Oil should be transparent and goldish.) The inside tread of the tires was bald, and on one tire I could see the steel belt coming through the surface of the rubber. That was just the visual inspection in the parking lot. When we got the vehicle into the shop, we found more than two-thousand-dollars' worth of safety items that needed to be addressed before it was road-worthy.

He was *extremely* lucky. Most dealerships would not have paid for after-sale repairs when the customer signs an "As Is" at closing. That is why it is so very, very important to have two things: a trusted ASE–Blue Seal shop and a vehicle inspection before purchasing a used vehicle.

Let's finalize your choice.

NOTES:

NOTES:

NOTES:

NOTES:

NOTES:

Chapter 9:

Buyer, beware!

You had your choice vehicle checked over before purchasing, right?

I cannot say this enough. Plumbers are proficient at plumbing, electricians know their way around a fuse panel, and ASE-certified technicians are vehicle savvy. Don't take anyone's word on the condition of your future vehicle. Don't go cheap and think that your high school auto shop class makes you qualified to check a vehicle over for purchase.

Now, another little-known trick is to have the vehicle checked out for vehicle identification number fraud. Thousands of vehicles are stolen each day. More than half are never recovered. They end up at a "chop shop" and are sold for parts. Or they get a new vehicle identification number (VIN) and become what are known as "cloned" cars. According to a local law enforcement source, Mexico is a very good source for new VIN plates. In all cars, there is a VIN plate on the dash and another on the inside of the driver's door. Some of these bogus plates are very good reproductions; others are obviously fraudulent. In one case shown to me, they could not spell the country of origin correctly. Our cousins to the north spell their country

C-A-N-A-D-A. The bogus plate spelled it C-A-N-B-D-A. You can spot these things when you know where to look for them.

A bogus VIN usually correlates to a vehicle that has already been destroyed at a salvage yard—and, in some cases, to a vehicle that was purchased from another source. This VIN is transferred from the original vehicle and placed on the hot car. If your used car happens to be one of these clone cars, and law enforcement performs a VIN check it and discovers the fraud, you lose possession. No compensation, no retribution; do not pass go, do not collect.

In one case, a law enforcement officer asked to have a vehicle hoisted on one of my vehicle lifts for inspection. The car was for sale at a major manufacturer dealership. The officer was right. It was a stolen, altered vehicle. Even the dealership had no idea—and, again, it was a major dealership. Even though you may have purchased it from a legit dealership, they could have been fooled by the VIN plate switch. This can happen to any of us. This switch could have occurred several owners before, but the person that has possession of the car at that time is the one who suffers the loss. Again, there is no compensation. Your car or truck is confiscated. Law enforcement just takes the car. Plain and simple.

To avoid this mess, have a law enforcement officer check to make sure the VIN is registered to that particular vehicle. Each car or truck has a separate VIN stamped on the frame, engine, and transmission. Also, each onboard computer has an identifier to the VIN of the vehicle. If something doesn't match, find out if something was legitimately exchanged or if possible fraud is involved.

72

Why take the chance?

There also are about half a dozen vehicle reporting sites that can tell you if a car or truck has been in an accident, flood, etc. Well, it can only report on what services were reported. Therefore, if the vehicle had a little fender-bender and the owner fixed it without reporting it to the insurance company, the repair will not show on the national report.

For example, a customer of mine decided to sell his high-priced European vehicle. I knew that the right front fender had been damaged in a minor accident. He did not turn in the mishap to the insurance company, but chose to pay for the repair. When it was time to sell the vehicle, the national data bases did not show the accident and repair. Instead it said the vehicle was "accident free"—far from the truth.

So, take information from these databases with a grain of salt. They can tell you only what was reported, not what actually happened in the life of the car. That's why it is particularly important to have your vehicle checked over by an independent, ASE-certified technician. This is what they do for a living. They know what to look for in and on an automobile. A technician would have been able to identify the body work on that fender and report it to the prospective buyer—something a national database missed. Now, not everyone is perfect, and some repair jobs are disguised very well, but at least, you will be have the opportunity to find out.

Now, let's get this ride financed.

NOTES:

NOTES:

NOTES:

NOTES:

Chapter 10:
Timing is everything

So, you've done your research and kicked more tires that you care to remember. You have found your dream car, and it is time to put a deposit on it. You know on any big purchase that it's wise to "sleep on it," to think it over. You don't want to make a rash decision because some salesperson pressured you into a purchase so he or she could meet a quota. This is your party, and you know what you want. There is no reason for someone to push you to make a rash decision that you may regret later.

For example, a customer of mine just had to have the latest model of a domestic vehicle. It was this car model's first sales month—a "gotta have it" vehicle. So the customer shopped at various dealerships within a seventy-five-mile radius. One afternoon, one of the dealership salesmen called the customer and said that he had a couple more vehicles come in, and one of them was the color the customer was requesting. Well, the customer went over to the dealership after work, and several hours later walked out with the new car.

Everything that the customer had planned for this purchase—bank financing, insurance, etc.—was thrown out the window. The salesperson got the customer to sign on to a lease that ultimately would have cost the customer more than ten thousand dollars extra. By the time the new car owner got home and his head stopped swimming, he came back to reality and called the dealership. The salesperson told the customer that he could not return the car—he was stuck. But he did alter the financing only back to what was agreed on in the original visit.

Remember, don't let salespeople push you. If you don't understand—stop! Ask a lot of questions until you comprehend what the salesperson is telling you. And if he is rude about it, there are other dealerships with other vehicles out there.

So, let's get back to the deposit. If you have all your ducks in a row, you do not have to go through the stress that this man experienced that evening. Be a good scout. Be prepared.

Make sure your deposit is refundable. You are making the deposit to hold onto a product that you are almost sure you want. But you need to think about the pros and cons of the purchase. Don't take for granted that the dealership you are working with is going to give you your money back. A lot of dealerships consider the deposit to be a rental fee—it just takes the vehicle off the potential vehicle purchase list. If you change your mind and don't want the car or truck— and you haven't confirmed that your deposit is a refundable deposit—you could lose that hard-earned money. And, at the same time, the car dealer can turn around and sell the vehicle to someone that had test driven it hours beforehand. They just made money off your little contribution.

Oh, and by the way, the best way to make a deposit on a vehicle is via a check or credit card—*no cash*. With either one of these options, you have a record of your deposit. If you change your mind and what your deposit back, you have a record of the deposit. If the dealer loses the deposit receipt, you have your own copy to fall back on.

What could you do with one hundred or five hundred dollars?

NOTES:

NOTES:

NOTES:

NOTES:

NOTES:

Chapter 11:

Have the auto buying advantage

So you want the vehicle. It's time to give the dealer the money to pay for it. But what type of financing will you choose? There are all types: bank loans, loans from friends or family, or dealership loans—and they all need to be investigated. You will have to let the lender know how much you plan for a down payment and then figure how many months you want to spread out the loan. The average is sixty months (five years), but car loans can go as longer. The more time you take to pay it off, the more the vehicle will cost.

It is up to you as a responsible car owner to determine what is right for you.

There are dozens of payment factor calculators that can tell you how much your payments will be, depending on the time and the percentage rate. And don't forget your insurance, as you want to know how the total amount you will be spending on this car or truck for your monthly budget.

How much will your insurance cost you for this new used vehicle? Well, it's time to call your insurance company and find out. They are going to need the vehicle identification number. Ask the car salesperson for this info when you make your deposit. The VIN will tell the insurance agent all the options on that particular vehicle. Every safety option on your new ride is money in your pocket. Make sure that you get credit for it.

And add fuel costs. You can't count on the posted miles per gallon (MPG) per vehicle. Fuel economy depends on your driving habits (fast starts from traffic signals; short stops at stop lights and signs, etc.) and where you live. City driving MPG can be very different from rural road MPG. Also, mountainous terrain or driving in extremely hot weather or extremely cold weather will make a difference. Using your present vehicle as a guide will give you a ballpark estimate on fuel costs.

Let's move from the test drive to the purchase.

NOTES:

NOTES:

NOTES:

NOTES:

NOTES:

Chapter 12:

And a lot of paperwork too

So you are ready to pull the trigger and purchase you dream machine. Before entering the dealership to close the sale, you need support documents. First you need your driver's license. You can purchase a vehicle with a valid state identification card, but you will not be able to drive the car off the lot. You will also need proof of insurance coverage for the new ride. Also, if you are going with outside financing (such as a bank), that paperwork will need to be in place before you can sign on the dotted line.

Some items will take a day or two to compile. The insurance shouldn't take too long. Just contact your agent and give her the details for transferring the insurance from your old vehicle to your new ride. This usually requires just a five-minute conversation over the telephone. The agent will need to e-mail or fax proof of coverage to the dealership before your purchase. This is an item that you may want to get out of the way early in the transaction.

Now, get that pen ready; it's time for the paperwork. And there is a lot of it! It's important to see each document that you sign. And *do not* sign your decisions away by putting your signature on power of attorney paper to have someone else make your choices. Why allow others to make legal decisions for you? How would you know if one piece of paper had a different odometer reading than the other? Your signature is the most powerful item you will every own. Protect it!

Again, there is a forest full of papers to sign. Each state has different rules, but you will be required to sign the items of your particular state—or the state that you are purchasing the vehicle in. Read *all* the text of each one carefully. Do not go off someone's interpretation of what they think or off what you to think is included in the text of each document. And having someone talk while you are reading—forget it! Tell them that you want time to read and ask them to talk to someone else in another room. You want to make sure you understand what you are signing.

I had a customer who didn't read the paperwork all the way through and thought that he was purchasing a vehicle. When he got home, he realized that he purchased a vehicle *lease*. Big difference! Big money!

You should receive copies of all the paperwork you signed. If you don't, ask for it. This should not be an issue. If it is, contact the sales manager, who should make things right.

One of the most important items that you will put your signature on is the one that states or implies a warranty on the vehicle you are purchasing. Is there a remaining factory warranty? Is there an aftermarket warranty? Or is the vehicle an "as is" with no warranty? And don't let them tell you that you need to purchase an aftermarket warranty when you purchase the car—and that you must do it *now*.

Wrong!

There are dozens and dozens of aftermarket vehicle warranties out there. You can do your homework beforehand and choose a handful of companies that suit your needs. Or wait until you actually make your purchase to choose the best fit for your new ride. You do not have to purchase aftermarket vehicle warranty when purchasing your used car. And why would you purchase an aftermarket warranty when the vehicle you chose has time left on its original, manufacturer warranty? All aftermarket warranties play second fiddle to the manufacturer's warranty. Purchasing a second warranty when you buy is just a waste of money for you and a financial gain for the dealership. Remember, not only does the dealership get money, but the salesperson gets money off the aftermarket warranty. That's why they push so hard. It takes money out of your wallet and into their bank account. Think about it before you buy it!

And strike while the iron is hot. You will always have the upper hand when negotiating a vehicle sale price the last day of the month or of a fiscal quarter or—better yet—on New Year's Eve. That's right. The ball is in your court when it comes to bargaining the final sale price. You want to buy a vehicle. The car dealer wants to sell a vehicle. It's the last day of the month, and he would like to have that extra sale on their books for the month. It's a win-win situation getting you into the car of your choice for the least amount of money.

Let's go for a ride in your new wheels.

NOTES:

NOTES:

NOTES:

NOTES:

Chapter 13:

*Keep it nice to keep
it (almost) forever*

True story: A couple was purchasing a vehicle for their teenage daughter. While the parents were busy reading and signing paperwork, the young female was busy on her smart phone. Not only did she find a photo of her new wheels, she posted the picture to her social media site to show off her new acquisition to more than a thousand of her friends and relatives.

Americans love their cars.

You just purchased either a new or used vehicle. Now is the time to start keeping your car or truck looking and running like the day you picked it up from the showroom.

First, a clean car has a happy owner. When you approach your vehicle in a parking lot or driveway, it is much more appealing than one that has bug guts splattered all over the front bumper and windshield, isn't it? So, wash your vehicle regularly. Not only does it keep the finish nice, but you will be more positive toward needed repairs. Another thing: fast-food bags are best stored in a trash receptacle—not inside your car. Yuck!

Go to a self-service car wash and throw a couple of coins into the vacuum. Vacuum not only the floor, but the seats too. You wouldn't believe the stuff that comes out of the seats. If you are quick about it, don't forget to vacuum the trunk too. The trunk is a place to transport objects; don't store unnecessary items in it. A trunk filled with a couple of bowling balls and a set of golf clubs just decreases your vehicle's fuel efficiency. It's not worth the price, considering today's fuel costs.

Have your tire pressure and fluid levels topped off every month. Choose a day of the month (I tell people to choose their birthday, like the twentieth), and go to your ASE–Blue Seal Shop to have this service performed. This does not require an appointment and takes less than ten minutes. Also, there should be no charge for this service. If they ask for money, find another shop.

And don't forget the oil change and tire rotation. These are two of the most important maintenance items for your vehicle. An ASE-certified technician performing the service can spot trouble brewing and fix the problem while it's minor, meaning the repair bill will be inconsequential. If there is something starting to smolder, you can fix the problem in the early stages.

Remember, if you don't like your vehicle, that's when mechanical problems occur. Think about it. If it makes a little noise, that's just something else you can "moan and groan" about. Well, that new noise is the beginning of a little something. And that little something can balloon into something larger if it isn't addressed. (We call that a domino effect. And, yes, it happens on cars and trucks too.) That extra money you are going to spend on the bigger repair could have gone as a down payment on a newer used vehicle—or a new car or truck. Plus, the neglect just decreases your vehicle's resale value. In other words, maintain your vehicle, because it will pay off in the end.

Here's the whole premise behind this book: I want you to be a savvy car consumer. I want you to go out and look at your vehicle, sitting in the driveway, and say, "Hey, I really like this car."

NOTES:

NOTES:

NOTES:

NOTES:

NOTES:

Acknowledgments

I would like to thank my family and friends for their support. And let's not forget my customers—without all your questions, there wouldn't be a Car Care for the Clueless series.

21129390R00063

Made in the USA
Lexington, KY
28 February 2013